Peculiarities of the life and reproduction of the Anhinga bird

Chapter 1: Introduction

Chapter 1: Background and purpose of the book Welcome to "Peculiarities of the life and reproduction of the Anhinga bird"! As an ornithologist, I have spent years studying the behavior, ecology, and morphology of this fascinating bird. The Anhinga, also known as the "snakebird" or "water turkey," is a unique and beautiful species that is found in wetlands throughout the Americas. Background on the Anhinga bird Anhingas are large, long-necked birds that are well-adapted to life in and around water. They have a distinctive appearance, with a slender body, long pointed bill, and black or dark brown feathers that are iridescent in sunlight. Unlike most water birds, Anhingas do not have oil glands on their feathers, which makes them more buoyant but less waterproof. This means they have to dry their wings after diving to hunt for fish, their primary food source. Purpose of the book The purpose of this book is to provide a comprehensive overview of the life and reproduction of the Anhinga bird. We will cover everything from their physical characteristics and behavior to their habitat selection and conservation status. Through this book, I hope to share my passion for this amazing bird with you and to raise awareness about the importance of protecting their habitats. Why study the Anhinga bird? Studying the Anhinga bird is important for several reasons. First, they are a fascinating species with unique adaptations for life in and around water. By learning more about their behavior and morphology, we can gain insights into the evolution of aquatic birds in general. Second, Anhingas are an important indicator species for wetland health. Their presence and abundance can tell us a lot about the quality of wetland habitats and the impacts of human activities on these ecosystems. Finally, Anhingas are also culturally significant in many parts of their range, with traditional stories and beliefs associated with their behavior and appearance. Conclusion In conclusion, this book aims to provide a comprehensive overview of the life and reproduction of the Anhinga bird. Through exploring their physical characteristics, behavior, and ecology, we hope to increase understanding and appreciation of this unique species. Furthermore, we hope to raise awareness of the importance of conserving wetland habitats, not only for the Anhinga bird but for the countless other species that depend on these ecosystems.

Chapter 2: Overview of the Anhinga bird and its habitat As an ornithologist, I have had the pleasure of observing and studying the Anhinga bird in its natural habitat. In this chapter, we will provide an overview of the Anhinga bird and its habitat, including its range, habitat preferences, and behavior. Range and distribution The Anhinga bird is found throughout the Americas, from the southeastern United States to Argentina. They are most commonly found in wetlands such as marshes, swamps, and rivers, but can also be found in coastal areas and freshwater lakes. Habitat preferences Anhingas are highly adapted to life in and around water. They are often found perched on branches or other structures near the water's edge, where they can easily spot their prey. They prefer habitats with dense vegetation and plenty of fish, but are also known to forage in open water. Behavior Anhingas are skilled divers and swimmers, using their long necks and sharp bills to catch fish and other aquatic prey. They are also known for their distinctive "drying" behavior, where they spread their wings and hold them outstretched to dry after diving. This behavior is necessary because Anhingas do not have oil glands on their feathers like most water birds, which makes them less waterproof. Threats and conservation The Anhinga bird faces a number of threats, including habitat loss and degradation, pollution, and human disturbance. Wetlands are one of the most threatened ecosystems in the world, with many wetland habitats being destroyed or degraded by human activities. Conservation efforts are underway to protect and restore wetlands and to raise awareness of the importance of these ecosystems. Conclusion In conclusion, the Anhinga bird is a fascinating species that is highly adapted to life in and around water. Its habitat preferences, behavior, and range make it an important indicator species for wetland health. However, the Anhinga bird and its habitat face many threats, and conservation efforts are necessary to protect and restore wetlands for the benefit of the Anhinga bird and countless other species.

Chapter 3: Importance of studying the Anhinga bird As an ornithologist, I have come to appreciate the importance of studying the Anhinga bird. In this chapter, we will explore some of the reasons why studying the Anhinga bird is important. Indicator species for wetland health The Anhinga bird is an important indicator species for wetland health. Wetlands are among the most productive ecosystems on Earth and provide a wide range of ecosystem services, including water purification, flood control, and carbon sequestration. However, wetlands are also among the most threatened ecosystems on the planet, with many wetland habitats being destroyed or degraded by human activities. Because the Anhinga bird is so dependent on wetlands for its survival, it can serve as an important indicator of wetland health. By monitoring Anhinga populations, we can gain insights into the health of wetland ecosystems and identify potential threats and conservation needs. Role in the food web Anhinga birds play an important role in the food web of wetland ecosystems. As piscivores, they feed primarily on fish, but will also consume other aquatic prey such as crustaceans and amphibians. By controlling populations of these prey species, Anhinga birds help to maintain the balance of wetland ecosystems. Conservation value Finally, the Anhinga bird has significant conservation value. As a wetland-dependent species, it is particularly vulnerable to habitat loss and degradation. By studying Anhinga populations and identifying threats to their habitat, we can develop effective conservation strategies to protect not only the Anhinga bird, but also the wetland ecosystems upon which it depends. Conclusion In conclusion, the Anhinga bird is an important species with significant conservation value. Studying the Anhinga bird can provide valuable insights into wetland health and ecosystem functioning, and can help us to develop effective conservation strategies to protect these important ecosystems.

Chapter 2: Morphology and Anatomy

Chapter 4: Physical characteristics of the Anhinga bird As an ornithologist, I have had the opportunity to closely observe the physical characteristics of the Anhinga bird. In this chapter, we will explore the unique physical features that make the Anhinga bird so well adapted to its aquatic lifestyle. Size and shape The Anhinga bird is a medium-sized bird, with males typically measuring between 85-95 cm in length and females measuring between 75-90 cm. They have a long, slender neck and a sharply pointed bill, which they use to spear their prey. Their bodies are streamlined and covered in waterproof feathers, allowing them to move easily through the water. Feathers and coloration The feathers of the Anhinga bird are uniquely adapted to its aquatic lifestyle. Unlike most birds, which have oil glands that secrete oil to waterproof their feathers, the Anhinga bird has feathers with a special structure that allows them to remain buoyant and dry. These feathers are also less dense than other bird feathers, which allows the Anhinga bird to dive more easily. The coloration of the Anhinga bird is also noteworthy. Adult males have glossy black feathers with white streaks on their wings, while females and juveniles have brown feathers with white speckles. The head and neck of both males and females are a distinctive blue-gray color. Legs and feet The Anhinga bird has long, powerful legs and webbed feet that are well adapted to swimming and diving. They use their legs to propel themselves through the water, while their webbed feet provide them with stability and maneuverability. Conclusion In conclusion, the physical characteristics of the Anhinga bird are uniquely adapted to its aquatic lifestyle. Its long, slender neck, sharply pointed bill, streamlined body, waterproof feathers, and webbed feet all allow it to move with ease through the water and hunt its prey.

Chapter 5: Skeletal structure and adaptations for diving As an ornithologist, I am fascinated by the skeletal structure and adaptations of the Anhinga bird that allow it to dive and swim so effectively. In this chapter, we will explore the unique features of the Anhinga bird's skeleton and musculature that make it such an efficient underwater hunter. Skeletal structure The Anhinga bird's skeletal structure is well adapted to its aquatic lifestyle. Its bones are hollow, which makes them lighter and more buoyant in the water. The neck vertebrae are also longer and more flexible than those of most other birds, which allows the Anhinga bird to bend and twist its neck to spear its prey. Adaptations for diving The Anhinga bird has several adaptations that make it an excellent diver. One of these adaptations is its ability to control the amount of air in its body. When diving, the Anhinga bird compresses its lungs and closes its glottis to prevent water from entering its respiratory system. It also reduces blood flow to non-essential organs, such as its digestive system, in order to conserve oxygen. Another adaptation is the placement of its legs and feet. The Anhinga bird's legs are set far back on its body, which allows it to swim and dive with greater efficiency. Its feet are also webbed, which provides additional propulsion and maneuverability in the water. Musculature The Anhinga bird's musculature is also well adapted to its aquatic lifestyle. Its pectoral muscles, which are responsible for powering its wings, are relatively small and weak compared to those of other birds. This is because the Anhinga bird primarily swims and dives rather than flying. Its leg muscles, on the other hand, are large and powerful, which allows it to propel itself through the water with ease. Conclusion In conclusion, the Anhinga bird's skeletal structure and adaptations for diving are remarkable examples of how animals can evolve to thrive in different environments. Its hollow bones, flexible neck vertebrae, ability to control air intake, webbed feet, and specialized musculature all make it an incredibly efficient underwater hunter.

Respiratory and Circulatory Systems of the Anhinga Bird

As an ornithologist, I find the respiratory and circulatory systems of the Anhinga bird to be particularly fascinating. These systems have undergone adaptations to allow the bird to be an efficient underwater hunter, catching fish and other prey in freshwater and saltwater habitats.

Respiratory System

Unlike other birds that have a bony structure called the syrinx located at the base of the trachea, the Anhinga bird has a more flexible trachea and a specialized larynx that allows it to completely close off its airway when diving. This adaptation allows the bird to dive underwater for extended periods of time without the risk of water entering its lungs.

The Anhinga bird also has a large air sac that extends from the lungs to the back of the body. This air sac acts as a buoyancy control device, allowing the bird to adjust its buoyancy while swimming and diving.

Circulatory System

The Anhinga bird has a highly efficient circulatory system that allows it to withstand the physiological stresses of diving. During a dive, the bird's heart rate slows down, and blood flow is redirected to the brain, heart, and other vital organs to conserve oxygen.

The bird's blood also contains a high concentration of hemoglobin, which is the protein that carries oxygen in the blood. This adaptation allows the bird to efficiently transport oxygen to its muscles and other tissues, even when diving for long periods of time.

In conclusion, the Anhinga bird has undergone fascinating adaptations to its respiratory and circulatory systems to allow it to be an efficient underwater hunter. These adaptations have helped the bird to thrive in its aquatic habitat, and studying them can give us insights into the amazing diversity of life on our planet.

Muscles and Movement

As an ornithologist, I have studied the fascinating anatomy of the Anhinga bird, which includes unique adaptations for movement and hunting. One of the most interesting aspects of the Anhinga's physical structure is its musculature.

The Anhinga bird has strong, powerful muscles in its neck and upper body that allow it to quickly and accurately strike at prey while swimming. These muscles are essential for the bird's hunting strategy, which involves diving beneath the surface of the water to catch fish and other small aquatic animals.

In addition to its neck and upper body muscles, the Anhinga also has strong leg muscles that it uses to propel itself through the water. The bird's legs are positioned far back on its body, which gives it excellent maneuverability and helps it to swim quickly and efficiently.

Another interesting aspect of the Anhinga's musculature is its wing structure. Unlike many other bird species, the Anhinga has relatively weak pectoral muscles, which means that it is not able to sustain flight for long periods of time. However, this adaptation allows the bird to swim more easily and efficiently, which is essential for its hunting strategy.

Overall, the Anhinga's unique musculature plays a crucial role in its ability to move and hunt effectively. By studying the bird's anatomy and physiology, we can gain a greater understanding of the adaptations that have allowed it to thrive in its aquatic habitat.

Chapter 3: Behavior and Ecology

As an ornithologist studying the Anhinga bird, it is important to understand their behavior and ecology. The Anhinga bird is a unique species that has adapted to living in and around water sources.

Behavior

Anhingas are solitary birds and are typically found alone or in small groups. They are known for their distinct swimming style, which involves their bodies being almost completely submerged with only their long neck and head visible above the water. Anhingas use their sharp beaks to catch fish and other prey underwater.

Their mating behaviors are also interesting to observe. During the breeding season, male Anhingas perform elaborate courtship displays to attract females. These displays involve spreading their wings and tail feathers and making a variety of sounds.

Ecology

The Anhinga bird is found in a variety of habitats, including freshwater marshes, swamps, and lakes. They can also be found near coastal areas and in mangrove swamps. They are found throughout the southeastern United States, as well as in Central and South America.

Anhingas are important indicators of the health of their ecosystems. They are sensitive to changes in water quality and habitat degradation. Monitoring the populations of Anhingas can provide valuable information about the overall health of an ecosystem.

The Anhinga bird also plays an important role in the food chain. As top predators in their habitats, they help regulate the populations of smaller fish and other prey species. They are also preyed upon by larger predators such as alligators and snakes.

Overall, understanding the behavior and ecology of the Anhinga bird is important for conservation efforts and for maintaining the balance of their ecosystems.

Diet and Foraging Behavior

The Anhinga bird is known for its unique feeding behavior, which involves spearing fish with its sharp beak while swimming underwater. This bird species primarily feeds on small to medium-sized fish, but may also consume crustaceans, amphibians, and even small reptiles.

The Anhinga's foraging behavior involves swimming with its head and neck submerged in water, using its webbed feet to propel itself forward. When the bird spots prey, it thrusts its long, pointed beak into the water to spear the fish. The Anhinga then lifts its head out of the water and tosses the fish into the air, catching it with its beak and swallowing it whole.

As an ornithologist, I find the Anhinga's feeding behavior to be fascinating and unique among bird species. It is also interesting to note that the Anhinga is able to dive to great depths in order to catch fish, thanks to its specialized skeletal and respiratory adaptations.

The Anhinga's diet and foraging behavior can have important ecological implications, as it plays a role in regulating fish populations in its habitat. The Anhinga is also an important food source for predators such as alligators, eagles, and other large birds.

Overall, understanding the Anhinga's diet and foraging behavior is important for studying its ecological role and for developing conservation strategies to protect this unique bird species.

Habitat selection and migration patterns

As an ornithologist, I find the habitat selection and migration patterns of the Anhinga bird to be fascinating. These birds inhabit a wide range of aquatic habitats including freshwater, brackish, and marine environments. They are commonly found in areas with abundant vegetation such as mangroves, swamps, and lagoons. Anhingas are also known to frequent wetlands, ponds, and rivers. During the breeding season, Anhingas are often found in large colonies. These colonies can contain hundreds of nests and are usually located in trees or shrubs near water. The birds build their nests with sticks and leaves, and both the male and female take turns incubating the eggs. After hatching, the chicks are fed regurgitated fish by both parents. Anhingas are known for their impressive fishing skills, and they have unique adaptations that help them to catch fish. They have a long, pointed bill which they use to spear fish, and they also have a flexible neck which allows them to move their head quickly and efficiently underwater. Anhingas are also able to adjust their buoyancy, allowing them to dive deep and stay underwater for extended periods of time. In terms of migration patterns, Anhingas are found throughout the Americas and parts of Africa. In North America, they are found in the southeastern United States, Central America, and the Caribbean. During the winter months, some populations of Anhingas migrate southward to warmer climates, while others remain in their breeding range year-round. Overall, the habitat selection and migration patterns of the Anhinga bird are complex and fascinating. These birds have adapted to a wide range of aquatic habitats and have developed unique hunting techniques to catch their prey. As an ornithologist, I continue to be intrigued by the behavior and ecology of this remarkable species.

Social behavior and communication

Communication: Anhinga birds have a unique way of communicating with one another. They use a variety of sounds and physical displays to convey different messages. For example, during courtship, males produce a deep, guttural call to attract females. When alarmed or threatened, they emit a loud hissing sound or a series of croaks to warn others of danger. Additionally, they use body language, such as spreading their wings or making a threat display, to communicate.

Social behavior: Anhinga birds are usually solitary birds, but they can form small groups during the breeding season. They do not form flocks like many other bird species. During breeding, males engage in elaborate courtship displays to attract females. They will often perch on a branch near the water and spread their wings to show off their colorful plumage. Once they have paired up, they will work together to build a nest and raise their chicks.

During the non-breeding season, Anhingas may come together in larger groups to forage in areas with abundant prey. However, they are still relatively independent and do not exhibit the tight social bonds seen in other bird species.

Opinion: As an ornithologist, I find the communication and social behavior of Anhinga birds fascinating. Their unique vocalizations and displays allow them to convey complex messages to one another, and their solitary nature makes them stand out among other bird species. It is intriguing to see how their behavior changes during the breeding and non-breeding seasons, and how they adapt to different environments to find food and shelter.

Predation and Defense Mechanisms

As an ornithologist, I have studied the various predators that pose a threat to the Anhinga bird. These predators include alligators, crocodiles, snakes, raccoons, and eagles. Alligators and crocodiles are known to be the biggest predators of the Anhinga bird, especially during the nesting season. These reptiles prey on the vulnerable chicks and eggs, which are left unguarded by the parent birds. However, adult Anhinga birds are capable of defending themselves against these predators. They use their sharp beaks to poke at the eyes of the alligators or crocodiles that come too close to their nest. Snakes are another predator of the Anhinga bird, and they can be a significant threat to both the chicks and adult birds. However, adult Anhinga birds have been observed to exhibit unique defense mechanisms against snakes. When confronted by a snake, the Anhinga bird will raise its wings and expose the white feathers on its body. This is thought to startle the snake and give the bird time to escape. Raccoons are also known to prey on Anhinga birds, especially when they are roosting in trees at night. However, the Anhinga bird has evolved a unique adaptation to avoid being preyed upon by raccoons. They roost in trees with very thin branches that cannot support the weight of a raccoon, making it difficult for the raccoon to reach the birds. Eagles are another predator of the Anhinga bird, and they are known to prey on both the chicks and adult birds. However, the Anhinga bird has a unique way of avoiding eagle attacks. When an eagle is spotted flying overhead, the Anhinga bird will make a hissing sound and fluff up its feathers to make itself look bigger. This makes it difficult for the eagle to get a good grip on the bird, and often causes it to abandon its attack. In conclusion, the Anhinga bird faces many threats from various predators. However, it has evolved unique adaptations and defense mechanisms to protect itself and its offspring. Studying these adaptations and behaviors is crucial to understanding the ecological role of the Anhinga bird in its habitat.

Chapter 4: Reproduction and Parental Care

Breeding Biology and Courtship Behavior of the Anhinga Bird

As an ornithologist, I find the breeding biology and courtship behavior of the Anhinga bird to be fascinating. The breeding season for these birds typically begins in late winter or early spring. During this time, male Anhingas will establish breeding territories and begin attracting mates.

Courtship Behavior

Male Anhingas use a variety of behaviors to attract females, including vocalizations, displays of their wings and tail feathers, and nest-building. One particularly striking courtship behavior is the "wing salute," in which a male will stretch his wings out to their full length and lift them up over his back while pointing his bill towards the sky. This display is often accompanied by a low-pitched, guttural call.

Another interesting courtship behavior is the "stick ceremony." During this ritual, the male will gather sticks and offer them to the female, who will then use them to build or repair the nest. This behavior is thought to demonstrate the male's ability to provide for the female and their future offspring.

Nesting Behavior

Once a pair has formed, they will work together to construct a nest out of sticks, leaves, and other materials. Anhingas typically nest in colonies, with multiple pairs nesting in close proximity to one another. The nests are typically located in trees or shrubs near bodies of water.

After the nest is completed, the female will lay a clutch of 2-6 eggs. Both parents take turns incubating the eggs for around 25-30 days until they hatch.

Parental Care

Once the eggs hatch, both parents will take on the responsibility of caring for the chicks. Anhinga chicks are altricial, meaning they are born relatively undeveloped and rely heavily on their parents for food and protection. The parents will take turns leaving the nest to forage for food, primarily fish, which they will bring back to the nest to feed the chicks.

As the chicks grow, they become more active and will begin to explore the nest and surrounding area. Eventually, they will fledge and leave the nest, although they will continue to rely on their parents for food and protection for some time after fledging.

Conclusion

The breeding biology and courtship behavior of the Anhinga bird is a fascinating subject for study. From their intricate courtship rituals to their cooperative parenting, these birds exhibit a complex and highly adapted set of behaviors that allow them to successfully reproduce and raise their young.

Nesting habits and selection of nest sites

One of the most fascinating aspects of bird behavior is the construction of nests. The Anhinga bird is no exception, and their nesting habits are a remarkable sight to behold.

Nest construction

The Anhinga bird builds its nest using a combination of sticks, twigs, and other plant material. The male usually starts the construction, and the female finishes the process by adding softer materials such as leaves, moss, and grass.

The nest is built in a platform style, and it is typically located in a tree or shrub near water. The Anhinga bird may also build its nest in the middle of a small island or on a fallen log near the water's edge.

The nest building process usually takes a few weeks, and the nest can be up to 3 feet in diameter. The

Anhinga bird will often reuse its nest year after year, adding new materials to it each breeding season.

Nest site selection

The Anhinga bird is highly selective when it comes to choosing a nest site. They prefer to build their nests near water, which makes sense since they are fish-eating birds. They also prefer areas with plenty of vegetation, which provides good cover and protection from predators.

Interestingly, the Anhinga bird often selects nest sites that are close to other nesting birds. This behavior is known as colonial nesting and is seen in many other bird species as well. Colonial nesting can provide protection against predators, as well as increased opportunities for finding a mate.

Nesting habits

The Anhinga bird typically lays between 2 to 5 eggs, which are incubated by both parents for about a month. Once hatched, the chicks are fed by both parents and grow rapidly. They leave the nest at about 6 to 8 weeks of age and are independent soon after that.

The nesting season for the Anhinga bird varies depending on its location, but it usually takes place between February and July.

Conclusion

The nesting habits of the Anhinga bird are fascinating and complex. From nest construction to nest site selection and the rearing of young, these birds exhibit many interesting behaviors. Studying these behaviors can provide valuable insights into the ecology and biology of this remarkable bird species.

Incubation and Hatching of Eggs

As an ornithologist, I find the process of incubation and hatching of eggs to be fascinating. The Anhinga bird is known for laying a clutch of 2 to 5 eggs, and the incubation period lasts for about 25 to 30 days. During this period, the male and female Anhinga take turns incubating the eggs. One interesting fact about the incubation process of Anhinga eggs is that the parents do not use their bodies to keep the eggs warm. Instead, they use their bills to regulate the temperature of the eggs. They will hold the eggs in their bills and adjust the position of the eggs to maintain the optimal temperature. This behavior is thought to be an adaptation to the hot and humid environments in which they live. Once the eggs are ready to hatch, the parents will use their bills to crack the eggshells. This process takes a few hours, and the hatchlings will emerge one by one. The hatchlings are born naked and blind, with only a small amount of down feathers. The parents continue to care for the hatchlings, providing them with food and protection. It is important to note that during the hatching process, the parents must be careful not to damage the eggs. The eggs are fragile, and any damage to the shell can be fatal to the developing embryo. Therefore, the parents must be gentle yet precise when using their bills to crack the eggshells. In conclusion, the incubation and hatching of Anhinga eggs is a delicate and fascinating process. The use of bills for regulating temperature and cracking the eggshells is a unique adaptation to their environment. The parents must be careful during the hatching process to ensure the survival of their offspring.

Chick Development and Parental Care

Chick Development

As a ornithologist, I find the development of Anhinga chicks fascinating. After hatching, the chicks are naked and helpless, with their eyes closed. Over the course of a few days, their feathers start to grow, and their eyes open. They become more active and vocal, begging their parents for food. During the first week, the chicks are entirely dependent on their parents for food and warmth. The parents take turns brooding the chicks to keep them warm and protect them from predators. They also bring food to the nest, regurgitating small fish and other aquatic animals for the chicks to eat. As the chicks grow, their appetites increase, and the parents have to work harder to provide enough food. The chicks also become more mobile and start to move around the nest, flapping their wings and practicing their balance. By the third week, the chicks are almost as big as the adults, and their feathers have fully developed. They are now able to regulate their own body temperature and spend less time under the parents' wings. They still rely on their parents for food, however, and will continue to do so for several more weeks.

Parental Care

Anhingas are known for their cooperative breeding behavior, in which multiple adults help to raise the chicks. Both parents and sometimes other adult birds from previous broods will assist in feeding and caring for the chicks. The parents take turns incubating the eggs and brooding the chicks to keep them warm and protect them from predators. They also bring food to the nest, regurgitating small fish and other aquatic animals for the chicks to eat. In addition to providing food and warmth, the parents also play an important role in teaching the chicks essential survival skills. They show the chicks how to hunt for food and defend themselves from predators. Overall, the level of parental care and cooperation among Anhingas is impressive and plays a crucial role in the survival of the species. As a ornithologist, I am constantly amazed by the dedication and hard work of these birds in raising their young.

Chapter 5: Adaptations for Diving and Swimming

Feather structure and waterproofing

As an ornithologist, I find feathers to be one of the most fascinating aspects of birds. Feathers are a unique characteristic of birds, and they serve several important functions. Not only do feathers allow birds to fly, but they also help to regulate body temperature and provide waterproofing. Feathers are made up of a central shaft, or rachis, with barbs branching off from it. The barbs, in turn, have smaller branches called barbules. These barbules have tiny hooks that interlock with the barbules of adjacent barbs, creating a strong and flexible structure. This structure allows birds to create different shapes with their feathers to control their flight. Feathers also play a critical role in waterproofing. The interlocking structure of barbs and barbules creates a tight weave that helps to keep water out. Additionally, many birds have special glandular secretions that they use to preen their feathers, spreading the secretions over their feathers to make them more waterproof. Waterproofing is particularly important for birds like the Anhinga, which spend a lot of time in and around water. Anhingas have evolved specialized feathers that are more permeable to water than other birds. This allows them to dive deeper and swim more efficiently than other waterbirds. However, it also means that their feathers become soaked and heavy after swimming. To counteract this, Anhingas have developed a unique behavior known as "wing-drying." After diving for fish, Anhingas will perch in the sun with their wings spread open, allowing them to dry out and regain their buoyancy. In summary, feathers are an incredible adaptation that allows birds to fly and regulate their body temperature. Additionally, feathers provide waterproofing that is critical for waterbirds like the Anhinga. Understanding feather structure and waterproofing is important for understanding the unique adaptations that birds have developed to thrive in their environments.

Wing Structure and Hydrodynamics

As an ornithologist, I am fascinated by the wing structure and hydrodynamics of birds, including the Anhinga bird. The wings of birds are highly specialized for flight and allow them to achieve remarkable feats such as soaring, hovering, and diving.

The wings of the Anhinga bird are long and pointed, with a span of up to 4 feet. The primary feathers at the tips of the wings can be individually controlled, allowing the bird to make precise adjustments to its flight path. The secondary feathers are also important for flight, as they provide lift and stability. The wing structure of the Anhinga bird is designed for efficient flight, with minimal drag and maximum lift.

Hydrodynamics also plays a crucial role in the flight of birds. When birds swim, their wings become hydrofoils that generate lift and propulsion. The Anhinga bird is a skilled swimmer, using its wings to propel itself through the water in search of prey. The wings of the Anhinga bird are uniquely adapted for swimming, with a flattened shape that helps to reduce drag and increase lift.

The combination of the Anhinga bird's specialized wing structure and hydrodynamics allows it to fly efficiently and swim gracefully. Whether soaring high above the water or diving beneath it, the Anhinga bird is a marvel of avian engineering.

In conclusion, the wing structure and hydrodynamics of birds, including the Anhinga bird, are fascinating subjects of study for ornithologists. These adaptations allow birds to achieve remarkable feats of flight and swimming and are a testament to the incredible adaptability and versatility of birds as a class.

Eyesight and Underwater Vision

As an ornithologist studying the Anhinga bird, it is fascinating to observe how this species has adapted to their environment through their eyesight and underwater vision. Anhinga birds have excellent eyesight, which is critical for their hunting and survival. Their eyes are positioned on the sides of their head, giving them a wide field of vision that helps them spot prey from a distance. Anhingas also have a third eyelid, called a nictitating membrane, that covers their eyes and protects them while underwater. Moreover, the Anhinga bird's eyes are specifically adapted to help them hunt underwater. They have a flattened lens that allows them to see clearly both in the air and underwater. They can adjust the shape of their lens to focus on objects at different distances, giving them the ability to spot prey in murky waters. The Anhinga bird also has specialized sensory cells called oil droplets in their eyes that enhance their color vision. This adaptation is particularly useful in underwater environments where colors appear muted or distorted. In addition to their excellent eyesight, Anhinga birds have also developed remarkable underwater vision. They have the ability to open and close their nostrils, which allows them to hunt for fish and other prey while submerged. The Anhinga can stay underwater for several minutes while searching for prey due to their unique respiratory system. When they locate prey, they extend their long, sharp beaks and pierce their prey with their pointed bills. Overall, the Anhinga bird's eyesight and underwater vision are essential adaptations that allow them to thrive in their aquatic environment. Studying the adaptations of the Anhinga can provide valuable insights into how other aquatic bird species have evolved to survive and thrive in their unique environments.

Skeletal adaptations for swimming

As an ornithologist studying the peculiarities of the Anhinga bird, I cannot help but admire its remarkable skeletal adaptations for swimming. The Anhinga has a long, slender body and a relatively short neck, which is essential for its diving and swimming abilities. One of the most notable skeletal adaptations of the Anhinga is its unique vertebral column. The cervical vertebrae are elongated and have interlocking joints, which allow the bird to bend and twist its neck in various directions. This flexibility is necessary for catching fish underwater. The thoracic vertebrae are also modified to allow for efficient swimming. They are fused together to form a rigid structure, which helps the bird to maintain a streamlined shape while swimming. Additionally, the Anhinga has modified wings that aid in swimming. The wings are long and narrow, and the bones are thinner and lighter than those of other birds. This adaptation reduces the weight of the wings and makes them more hydrodynamic, allowing the bird to move through the water with minimal resistance. Another adaptation is the position of the legs. The Anhinga has its legs positioned far back on its body, which provides extra propulsion when swimming. The feet are also partially webbed, allowing the bird to maneuver and steer underwater. In my opinion, these skeletal adaptations of the Anhinga are fascinating and demonstrate the incredible adaptations that birds can develop to suit their unique environments. The Anhinga's adaptations for swimming make it a highly specialized and successful predator in aquatic ecosystems.

Chapter 6: Feeding Ecology

Diet Composition and Prey Selection

As an ornithologist studying the Anhinga bird, it is fascinating to observe its feeding behavior and prey selection. Anhingas are piscivorous, meaning they primarily feed on fish, but they also consume other aquatic animals such as crustaceans and amphibians.

The Anhinga has a long, slender, sharp bill which it uses to spear fish underwater. The bird's bill is perfectly adapted for this task, as it is pointed and has a serrated edge that helps it to grip slippery prey. In addition, the Anhinga's sharp bill allows it to kill its prey quickly and efficiently, minimizing the risk of injury from struggling fish.

Anhingas are also known for their unique feeding behavior. Unlike other waterbirds, they swim with their bodies submerged and their long necks and bills protruding from the water. This allows them to approach their prey without alerting them, increasing their chances of a successful catch.

The Anhinga's diet varies depending on the availability of prey. In some regions, they have been observed feeding on a variety of fish species such as catfish, tilapia, and cichlids. They also consume crayfish, shrimp, and other crustaceans. Interestingly, Anhingas are known to forage in both freshwater and saltwater environments.

As an ornithologist, it is important to understand the role of the Anhinga bird in its ecosystem. Anhingas are top predators in their aquatic habitats, and their diet can have a significant impact on the populations of their prey species. In addition, studying the Anhinga's diet can provide insights into the health and condition of the surrounding ecosystem.

In conclusion, the Anhinga's diet composition and prey selection is a fascinating area of study. Their unique feeding behavior and specialized bill make them efficient predators of aquatic animals, and their role in their ecosystem is an important one to consider.

Feeding behavior and techniques

As an ornithologist, I have studied the feeding behavior and techniques of many bird species, including the Anhinga. Anhingas are carnivorous birds that mainly feed on fish, but they also eat other small aquatic animals such as crustaceans and amphibians. Anhingas are skilled divers and hunters. They use their long, slender bills to spear fish underwater, and their sharp, backward-facing barbs prevent the prey from escaping. Anhingas are known to swim with only their necks and heads above water, while their bodies remain submerged. They do this to reduce water resistance and facilitate their hunting efforts. Once the Anhinga has caught its prey, it uses its bill to toss the fish into the air and then catch it headfirst. This behavior is thought to help the bird swallow the fish more easily. Anhingas are also known to exhibit cooperative feeding behavior. They may form groups and swim in a line, driving fish towards shallow water where they are easier to catch. They also cooperate with other bird species such as cormorants and herons, with each bird taking turns to dive and catch fish. In addition to their hunting techniques, Anhingas also have unique feeding habits. They lack oil glands and are unable to waterproof their feathers like other aquatic birds such as ducks and geese. As a result, Anhingas need to dry their feathers after diving underwater. They do this by perching on tree branches or other elevated structures with their wings spread out, a behavior known as "wing-drying". Overall, the feeding behavior and techniques of the Anhinga are impressive adaptations for a life in and around water. Their specialized bill and diving abilities make them efficient hunters, while their cooperative feeding behavior and wing-drying habits are important for survival.

Competition with other bird species

As an ornithologist, it is fascinating to observe the interactions between different bird species in their natural habitats. The Anhinga bird is known to face competition from various bird species for resources such as food and nesting sites.

Bird species that compete with the Anhinga for food:

- **Cormorants:** Cormorants are similar to Anhingas in many ways and feed on the same prey items, such as fish and small aquatic invertebrates. This can result in direct competition between the two species, especially in areas where food is scarce.
- **Egrets and herons:** These birds also feed on fish and other small aquatic animals, and are often found in the same habitats as Anhingas.

They may compete with Anhingas for access to feeding areas.

Bird species that compete with the Anhinga for nesting sites:

- **Wood storks:** Wood storks are large wading birds that often nest in colonies with other bird species, including Anhingas. This can lead to competition for suitable nesting sites, especially if there are limited resources available.

- **Ospreys:** Ospreys are another bird species that may compete with Anhingas for nesting sites. They prefer to build their nests on tall structures such as poles and trees, which are also favored by Anhingas.

Despite facing competition from other bird species, Anhingas have developed unique adaptations that allow them to thrive in their environments. Their ability to dive and swim underwater for extended periods of time, for example, gives them an advantage over other birds that cannot swim as well. Additionally, the Anhinga's sharp bill and keen eyesight allow it to accurately locate and catch prey.

Relationship with aquatic habitats

As an ornithologist studying the Anhinga bird, I have observed their strong relationship with aquatic habitats. These birds are highly adapted to living near and in water, with specialized physical and behavioral traits that allow them to thrive in such environments.

One of the key physical adaptations of the Anhinga bird is their long, slender neck. This allows them to reach deep into the water to catch fish and other prey. They also have strong, pointed bills that are ideal for spearing fish. In addition, their webbed feet and flattened tails make them excellent swimmers, allowing them to move through the water with ease.

Behaviorally, Anhingas are known for their habit of perching on branches overhanging the water with their wings spread open. This is not just a way to dry their wings, but also a way to regulate their body temperature. This is an important adaptation, as birds that live in or near water are constantly exposed to the cooling effects of evaporation. By spreading their wings, Anhingas increase the surface area of their bodies, which allows them to dissipate excess heat and stay cool.

Another interesting aspect of Anhinga behavior is their use of nesting sites near water. These birds typically build their nests in trees or shrubs near water, which provides them with easy access to food sources. This also makes it easier for them to transport food to their young, as they can simply fly from the water to their nest.

In addition to their physical and behavioral adaptations, Anhingas are also highly attuned to the characteristics of aquatic habitats. They tend to prefer shallow, slow-moving water with plenty of vegetation. This type of habitat provides them with a good supply of food, as well as shelter from predators. They are also able to find nesting sites near such water sources, which makes it easier for them to raise their young.

In conclusion, the Anhinga bird's strong relationship with aquatic habitats is a fascinating aspect of their biology. From their physical and behavioral adaptations to their preferences for certain types of water sources, these birds have developed a unique set of traits that allow them to thrive in these environments.

Chapter 7: Habitat Selection and Conservation

Habitat Preferences and Requirements

As an ornithologist studying the Anhinga bird, it is fascinating to observe their unique habitat preferences and requirements. These birds are native to the wetlands of the southeastern United States, Mexico, and Central and South America. They are often found in shallow, freshwater habitats such as swamps, marshes, and lakes. One interesting fact about the Anhinga bird is that they are able to adapt to a wide range of aquatic habitats. They can be found in both still and flowing waters, from small streams to large rivers. They also have the ability to tolerate a wide range of water conditions, from clear to murky and even polluted waters. While the Anhinga bird is adaptable to various aquatic habitats, there are some specific requirements that they need to thrive. They require a habitat with abundant fish populations as they are primarily fish-eaters. In addition to fish, they also consume amphibians, crustaceans, and insects, so a diverse range of prey is important to their survival. Another important requirement for the Anhinga bird is access to suitable nesting sites. They prefer to nest in trees located near water sources, and will often use the same nest site year after year. This highlights the importance of maintaining and preserving their natural habitat. Human activities such as development and pollution have impacted the Anhinga bird's habitat, making it difficult for them to find suitable nesting sites and healthy fish populations. Conservation efforts are crucial to ensure the survival of these birds, as well as the preservation of their habitat. In conclusion, the Anhinga bird's habitat preferences and requirements are unique and fascinating. They are adaptable to various aquatic habitats, but require access to suitable nesting sites and abundant fish populations to thrive. It is important for humans to be aware of the impact our activities have on their habitat and to work towards conservation efforts to ensure the survival of these magnificent birds.

Threats to the Anhinga bird and its habitats

As an ornithologist, I am aware of the various threats that the Anhinga bird faces in its natural habitat. These threats can range from natural causes to anthropogenic influences.

Natural threats

The Anhinga bird, like any other animal, is subjected to various natural threats such as predation, diseases, and natural disasters. One of the major predators of the Anhinga bird is the alligator, which is known to prey on both adults and juveniles. Other predators include snakes, raccoons, and eagles. These predators can have a significant impact on the Anhinga population, especially in areas where their natural habitats are being destroyed.

Moreover, diseases such as avian malaria and West Nile virus can also affect the Anhinga bird population. These diseases can be transmitted by mosquitoes, which are common in wetland habitats, where the Anhinga bird resides. Natural disasters such as hurricanes and floods can also have a significant impact on the Anhinga population by destroying their nests and reducing their food sources.

Anthropogenic threats

Human activities such as pollution, habitat destruction, and hunting also pose a significant threat to the Anhinga bird and its habitats. Pollution from industrial and agricultural activities can contaminate the water bodies where the Anhinga bird feeds, leading to the accumulation of toxins in their bodies. This can affect their reproductive success, growth, and survival.

Habitat destruction is also a significant threat to the Anhinga bird. Wetland habitats, where the Anhinga bird resides, are being destroyed to make way for human settlements, agriculture, and other human activities. This results in the fragmentation of their natural habitats, making it difficult for the Anhinga bird to find suitable nesting and feeding grounds. This can also lead to an increase in human-animal conflicts, as the Anhinga bird may venture into human settlements in search of food.

Hunting and poaching of the Anhinga bird for their meat, feathers, and bones also pose a significant threat to their population. Although hunting and poaching of the Anhinga bird are illegal in many countries, it still persists due to the high demand for their products in the black market.

Conclusion

The Anhinga bird and its habitats are facing various threats, both natural and anthropogenic. As ornithologists, it is our responsibility to raise awareness about these threats and work towards their conservation. This can be achieved through various measures such as habitat restoration, community education, and legal protection. By working together, we can ensure the survival of the Anhinga bird and its habitats for future generations to come.

Conservation efforts and management strategies

As an ornithologist, I am always concerned about the conservation of bird species and their habitats. The Anhinga bird, like many other bird species, faces several threats to its survival. Therefore, conservation efforts and management strategies are essential to ensure the long-term survival of the species. One of the most important conservation efforts is the protection and preservation of the Anhinga bird's habitats. Wetlands and freshwater habitats are critical to the survival of the species, and it is essential to ensure that these habitats remain healthy and intact. This can be achieved through habitat restoration, protection of wetlands, and regulation of human activities that may threaten the habitats. Another important conservation effort is the management of the Anhinga bird populations. This can be done through monitoring and research to determine population size, distribution, and health. The use of conservation genetics to study the genetic diversity of the populations is also crucial. These data can be used to develop effective management plans to ensure the long-term survival of the species. Conservation education is also an important strategy for the preservation of the Anhinga bird. Raising public awareness about the importance of the species and its habitats can help reduce human activities that may threaten the survival of the bird. Education can also help promote conservation policies and practices that benefit the species. The establishment of protected areas and the enforcement of wildlife protection laws are also crucial in the conservation of the Anhinga bird. Protected areas can provide safe habitats for the species, while wildlife protection laws can help prevent hunting, trade, and other activities that may harm the bird. In conclusion, the Anhinga bird, like many other bird species, faces numerous threats to its survival. However, with effective conservation efforts and management strategies, the species can be protected and preserved for future generations. As ornithologists, we have a responsibility to advocate for the conservation of bird species and their habitats, and to work towards a sustainable future for all living beings.

Future directions for research and conservation

As an ornithologist, I believe that there is still much to learn about the Anhinga bird and its behavior in the wild. Future research should focus on expanding our knowledge of their breeding biology, migration patterns, and genetic diversity. By understanding these aspects of their life cycle, we can better manage and conserve their populations.

Additionally, conservation efforts should continue to protect and preserve their natural habitats. This includes the implementation of regulations and policies to reduce habitat destruction and pollution, as well as the creation of protected areas for the Anhinga bird and other wildlife.

Another important aspect of conservation is educating the public about the ecological significance of the Anhinga bird and the threats they face. By raising awareness and promoting responsible behavior, we can encourage people to take action and contribute to the protection of these birds and their habitats.

Finally, I believe that continued collaboration between researchers, conservationists, and government agencies is essential for the long-term success of Anhinga bird conservation efforts. By working together, we can pool our knowledge and resources to develop effective strategies for protecting this unique and important species.

Chapter 8: Adaptations to Climate and Environment

Physiological adaptations to temperature and humidity

As an ornithologist studying the Anhinga bird, it's important to understand how these birds adapt to their environment. Temperature and humidity are two important factors that affect the Anhinga's behavior, reproduction, and survival.

Temperature Adaptations

The Anhinga bird is well adapted to living in warm environments. Their large wingspan and streamlined body shape allow them to efficiently dissipate excess body heat. Additionally, Anhingas have the ability to regulate their body temperature through panting and adjusting their metabolism. During hot weather, Anhingas will open their beaks and rapidly vibrate their throats, allowing moisture to evaporate from their mouths and airways, which helps cool their body temperature. This behavior is known as gular fluttering.

Humidity Adaptations

Anhingas are also adapted to humid environments. Their feather structure allows them to easily shed water and dry quickly. Their skin is also adapted to prevent water loss in humid environments. During breeding season, Anhingas build nests in trees near bodies of water. The high humidity around the water helps to keep the eggs and chicks hydrated.

Conclusion

The Anhinga bird has evolved several physiological adaptations to cope with high temperatures and humidity. These adaptations allow them to survive and thrive in their environment. Understanding these adaptations is crucial for conservation efforts and protecting the species in the face of environmental changes.

Responses to Extreme Weather Events

As an ornithologist studying the Anhinga bird, it's important to understand how these birds respond to extreme weather events such as hurricanes, droughts, and floods.

Hurricanes

Hurricanes can have devastating effects on bird populations, but Anhingas have developed adaptations to help them survive. During a hurricane, Anhingas will seek shelter in trees and hunker down until the storm passes. They may also fly to areas with calmer waters to avoid the high winds and rough waves. After a hurricane, Anhingas may face food shortages due to destruction of their habitat. However, they are able to disperse to other areas and adapt their feeding habits to find alternative food sources.

Droughts

Droughts can also have significant impacts on Anhinga populations. Anhingas rely on freshwater sources to find food, but during droughts, these sources may dry up or become too shallow for diving. To cope with droughts, Anhingas will search for alternative water sources, such as ponds or lakes that may have higher water levels. They may also switch to feeding on fish that live in shallower waters or even insects and other small prey.

Floods

Flooding can also impact Anhinga populations by washing away nests and disrupting breeding cycles. However, Anhingas have adapted to this by building nests in trees that are located higher above the water. In addition, flooding can also create new habitats for Anhingas. Flooded areas can provide an abundance of new food sources, and Anhingas may even use floating vegetation to build new nests.

Conclusion

Extreme weather events can have significant impacts on Anhinga populations, but these birds have developed a range of adaptations to help them survive. By understanding these responses to extreme weather events, we can better protect and conserve Anhinga populations in the face of environmental changes.

Effects of Habitat Degradation and Pollution

As an ornithologist studying the Anhinga bird, it's important to understand the effects of habitat degradation and pollution on their survival and reproduction.

Habitat Degradation

Anhingas rely on a specific habitat for their survival, which includes water bodies, wetlands, and trees. Habitat degradation can have a significant impact on their populations. When wetlands are drained for development or farming, Anhingas lose important feeding and nesting grounds. Destruction of trees through logging or urbanization can also reduce their nesting sites.

Pollution

Pollution is another threat to Anhinga populations. Water pollution can affect the quality of their food sources, making it more difficult for them to find suitable prey. Pesticides and other chemicals can also accumulate in their bodies and affect their reproduction and immune systems.

Conclusion

Habitat degradation and pollution are major threats to the survival of Anhinga populations. As ornithologists, it's our responsibility to advocate for conservation efforts to protect their habitats and reduce pollution. By working together, we can ensure the survival and well-being of these unique and important birds for future generations to enjoy.

Adaptations to Changing Environments

As an ornithologist studying the Anhinga bird, it's important to understand how these birds have adapted to changing environments over time.

Feeding Adaptations

Anhingas have developed a unique feeding strategy that has allowed them to adapt to changes in their environment. They are expert divers and can stay underwater for long periods of time in search of their prey. Anhingas also have a specialized beak that helps them catch and hold onto fish. Their beak is pointed and sharp, which allows them to easily penetrate through the scales of their prey. They also lack oil glands, which makes their feathers more permeable and allows them to dive more easily.

Nesting Adaptations

Anhingas build their nests in trees near water, and have developed adaptations to protect their nests from predators. They build their nests high up in the trees to make it more difficult for predators to reach. They also build their nests using sticks and other materials that are too large for smaller predators to move.

Migratory Adaptations

Anhingas have also developed migratory adaptations that allow them to move to different areas in response to changes in their environment. During the breeding season, Anhingas will travel to areas with suitable nesting sites and food sources. During the non-breeding season, they may migrate to areas with milder temperatures and more abundant food sources.

Conclusion

Anhingas have developed a range of adaptations to help them survive in changing environments. By understanding these adaptations, we can better protect and conserve their populations in the face of environmental changes. As ornithologists, it's our responsibility to continue studying and advocating for the conservation of these unique and important birds.

Chapter 9: Evolution and Phylogeny

Evolutionary History and Relationships with Other Bird Species

As an ornithologist studying the Anhinga bird, it's important to understand their evolutionary history and their relationships with other bird species.

Evolutionary History

Anhingas belong to the darter family, which is a group of fish-eating birds found in tropical and subtropical regions around the world. Fossil records suggest that the darter family has existed for over 30 million years. The Anhinga bird itself has a long evolutionary history, with evidence of their existence dating back over 20 million years. They have evolved to have long, slender bodies, which make them excellent divers and swimmers.

Relationships with Other Bird Species

Anhingas have a close relationship with other darter species, such as the Oriental Darter and the African Darter. They are also related to cormorants and pelicans, which are other fish-eating birds found in similar habitats. While they may share some similarities with other bird species, Anhingas have unique characteristics that set them apart. Their long, pointed beak and lack of oil glands distinguish them from other fish-eating birds.

Conclusion

Understanding the evolutionary history and relationships of the Anhinga bird is important for understanding their place in the natural world. As ornithologists, it's our responsibility to continue studying and learning about these unique and important birds. By doing so, we can better protect and conserve their populations for future generations to enjoy.

Genetic and Morphological Variation within the Anhinga Bird

As an ornithologist studying the Anhinga bird, it's important to understand the genetic and morphological variation within the species. This knowledge can help us better understand their biology, behavior, and evolution.

Genetic Variation

There is currently limited research on the genetic variation within Anhinga populations. However, studies suggest that there may be some genetic differences between different populations. For example, a study of Anhinga populations in Brazil found some genetic differentiation between populations in different river basins. Further research is needed to fully understand the genetic variation within Anhinga populations and its implications for the species.

Morphological Variation

Anhingas show some morphological variation, particularly in bill shape and size. In general, males have longer bills than females, and individuals in some populations may have larger bills than those in others. Morphological variation can be influenced by a variety of factors, such as diet and habitat. For example, individuals living in areas with larger fish may have evolved larger bills to better catch their prey.

Conclusion

Studying the genetic and morphological variation within the Anhinga bird can help us better understand the species and its evolution. While there is still much to learn, early research suggests that there may be some genetic and morphological differences between different populations of Anhingas. As ornithologists, it's important to continue studying and learning about the Anhinga bird and its unique characteristics. By doing so, we can better protect and conserve their populations for future generations to enjoy.

Phylogenetic Relationships and Classification of the Anhinga Bird

As an ornithologist studying the Anhinga bird, understanding its phylogenetic relationships and classification is important in order to understand its evolutionary history and its place in the broader context of bird taxonomy.

Phylogenetic Relationships

The Anhinga bird is part of the family Anhingidae, which includes four species: Anhinga anhinga (the Anhinga or American Darter), Anhinga novaehollandiae (the Australasian Darter), Anhinga rufa (the African Darter), and Anhinga melanogaster (the Oriental Darter). Phylogenetic studies suggest that the family Anhingidae is part of the clade Suliformes, which also includes other families such as the boobies and gannets.

Classification

The Anhinga bird is classified as part of the order Suliformes, family Anhingidae, and genus Anhinga. It is the only species in its genus. The Anhinga bird is also known by other common names, including the American Darter, Water Turkey, and Snakebird. Its scientific name, Anhinga anhinga, is derived from the Brazilian Tupi language and means "devil bird" or "snake bird," referring to its snake-like appearance when swimming with only its head and neck above water.

Conclusion

Understanding the phylogenetic relationships and classification of the Anhinga bird is important for understanding its evolutionary history and its place within the broader context of bird taxonomy. While there is still much to learn about the Anhinga bird and its relatives, early studies suggest that it is part of the clade Suliformes and is the only species in its genus. As ornithologists, it's important to continue studying and learning about the Anhinga bird and its unique characteristics in order to better protect and conserve its populations for future generations to enjoy.

Biogeographic history and diversification

As an ornithologist, understanding the biogeographic history and diversification of the Anhinga bird is essential to fully appreciate its unique characteristics.

Biogeography is the study of the distribution of species and how they have evolved over time. The Anhinga bird is found in the Americas, ranging from the southeastern United States to Argentina, and is a member of the darter family, Anhingidae.

Recent genetic studies have shed light on the biogeographic history of the Anhinga bird. These studies suggest that the family Anhingidae is a relatively young group of birds that arose in South America around 23 million years ago. The ancestors of the Anhinga bird likely originated in South America and dispersed northward into the Caribbean and southern North America.

Over time, the Anhinga bird evolved into several distinct subspecies, each with its unique characteristics. For example, the subspecies A. anhinga leucogaster, found in the southeastern United States and the Caribbean, has a white belly, while A. anhinga anhinga, found in South America, has a darker belly.

The diversification of the Anhinga bird is also thought to have been influenced by historical climate changes and geological events, such as the formation of the Isthmus of Panama, which occurred around three million years ago. This event allowed species from North and South America to mix, leading to new opportunities for the Anhinga bird to adapt and evolve.

Overall, the biogeographic history and diversification of the Anhinga bird provide valuable insights into the evolutionary processes that have shaped this fascinating species.

Chapter 10: Conclusion

Summary of the Main Findings and Conclusions

Throughout this book, we have explored the peculiarities of the life and reproduction of the Anhinga bird. From their physiological adaptations to extreme temperatures and humidity, to their responses to weather events, and their adaptations to changing environments, we have gained a deeper understanding of these fascinating creatures.

We have also examined the effects of habitat degradation and pollution on the Anhinga bird, and the genetic and morphological variations within the species. Additionally, we have explored their evolutionary history, biogeographic history, and classification, providing insight into the broader context of their existence.

Through this comprehensive analysis, we can draw several conclusions about the Anhinga bird. Firstly, their remarkable physiological adaptations allow them to survive in extreme environments, highlighting the adaptability of these birds. Secondly, they exhibit remarkable resilience in response to weather events, though habitat degradation and pollution pose significant threats to their existence.

Furthermore, genetic and morphological variations within the species suggest that further research is required to fully understand the diversity of Anhinga birds. Additionally, their biogeographic history and diversification illustrate their complex evolutionary journey and highlight the importance of their conservation.

Overall, our analysis of the Anhinga bird reveals a complex and fascinating species with unique biological and ecological traits. It is our hope that this book will inspire further research into these birds and facilitate the development of strategies for their conservation and protection.

Future Directions for Research on the Anhinga Bird

As an ornithologist, I am keenly aware that our knowledge of the Anhinga bird is far from complete. There is still much that we do not know about this fascinating species, and there are many avenues for future research that hold great promise for deepening our understanding of these birds and their place in the natural world.

1. Behavioral Ecology

One area that warrants further investigation is the behavioral ecology of the Anhinga bird. This includes the study of their foraging behavior, social interactions, mating behavior, and parental care. By better understanding these aspects of their behavior, we can gain insights into how they have adapted to their environment and how they might respond to changes in their habitat or other external factors.

2. Population Dynamics

Another important area of research is the population dynamics of the Anhinga bird. This includes the study of their demographics, population growth rates, and factors that influence their reproductive success. By monitoring the size and health of Anhinga populations over time, we can assess the health of their habitats and identify potential threats to their survival.

3. Genetics and Evolution

Advances in genetic and molecular techniques have opened up new avenues for understanding the evolutionary history and genetic diversity of the Anhinga bird. By analyzing their DNA, we can investigate their relationships with other bird species and gain insights into their evolutionary history. We can also study the genetic basis of traits such as plumage color, bill shape, and body size, which can provide clues about how these birds have adapted to their environment over time.

4. Conservation

The Anhinga bird is listed as a species of least concern by the International Union for Conservation of Nature (IUCN), but they still face threats from habitat loss, pollution, and hunting. Further research is needed to identify the specific threats to Anhinga populations and develop strategies to mitigate these threats. This could include habitat restoration, captive breeding programs, and public education campaigns to raise awareness about the importance of protecting these birds and their habitats.

Conclusion

The Anhinga bird is a remarkable species with many unique adaptations and behaviors that make them fascinating to study. By continuing to explore their biology, behavior, and ecology, we can deepen our understanding of these birds and gain insights into the broader ecological and evolutionary processes that shape the natural world. I look forward to seeing the exciting discoveries that emerge from future research on the Anhinga bird.

Implications for Understanding the Ecology and Evolution of Other Bird Species

Studying the ecology and evolution of a single bird species such as the Anhinga can provide valuable insights into the broader patterns of avian diversity. By examining the adaptations and behaviors of the Anhinga, we can begin to understand how similar species may have evolved and adapted to their respective environments.

Ecological Implications

The Anhinga is an excellent model species for examining the ecology of wetland birds. Their dependence on fish as a primary food source makes them particularly sensitive to changes in aquatic environments, and understanding their behavior and resource use can provide insights into the functioning of wetland ecosystems.

Furthermore, the Anhinga's nesting habits can shed light on the interactions between bird species and their environments. By studying how the Anhinga selects and constructs its nesting sites, we can gain a better understanding of how other bird species may adapt to their own unique nesting environments.

Evolutionary Implications

Studying the evolutionary history of the Anhinga can also provide insights into the broader patterns of avian evolution. The Anhinga belongs to the order Suliformes, which also includes other species such as cormorants and frigatebirds.

Comparing the morphology, behavior, and genetic makeup of the Anhinga with these other species can provide clues about their shared evolutionary history and the selective pressures that have shaped their diversification. Furthermore, understanding the factors that have led to the diversification of the Anhinga itself can provide insights into the processes driving avian diversification more broadly.

Conclusion

The Anhinga bird is a unique and fascinating species that has much to offer in terms of our understanding of avian ecology and evolution. By studying this species in depth, we can gain valuable insights into the functioning of wetland ecosystems and the processes that have driven the diversification of avian life.

As ornithologists, it is our duty to continue studying the Anhinga and other bird species to deepen our understanding of the natural world and inform efforts to conserve and protect these incredible animals for future generations.

Final thoughts and reflections

As an ornithologist who has studied the Anhinga bird extensively, I am struck by the many fascinating aspects of its life history and behavior. From its unique feeding strategy to its elaborate courtship displays, this bird is truly one of a kind. However, my research on the Anhinga also highlights the importance of understanding the ecological and evolutionary context in which it exists. As we continue to study and learn about the Anhinga bird, it is clear that its conservation is of utmost importance. Habitat loss, pollution, and other human impacts are threatening this species and many others like it. It is our responsibility as scientists, conservationists, and citizens of the planet to take action to protect these vulnerable creatures and the ecosystems in which they live. I believe that the Anhinga bird is not only a fascinating species in its own right, but also serves as a valuable model for understanding the ecology and evolution of other bird species. By studying the Anhinga and its adaptations to changing environments, we can gain insight into the strategies that other birds have used to survive and thrive in different habitats. In closing, I would like to emphasize the importance of continued research on the Anhinga bird and other species like it. Through our investigations, we can deepen our understanding of the natural world and work to preserve its wonders for generations to come.

www.ingramcontent.com/pod-product-compliance
Lightning Source LLC
Chambersburg PA
CBHW051754250726
48659CB00001B/418